# THE ANIMA
## OF PAUL BOWLES

Also by Karren LaLonde Alenier:

*On a Bed of Gardenias: Jane & Paul Bowles*, 2012

*The Steiny Road To Operadom: The Making Of American Operas*, 2007

*Gertrude Stein Invents a Jump Early On*, 2005

*Karren LaLonde Alenier Greatest Hits 1973–2002*, 2003

*Looking for Divine Transportation*, 1999

*Bumper Cars: Gertrude Said She Took Him for a Ride*, 1996

*The Dancer's Muse*, 1981

*Wandering on the Outside*, 1975

# THE ANIMA
# OF PAUL BOWLES

## Karren LaLonde Alenier

MadHat Press
Asheville, North Carolina

MadHat Press
MadHat Incorporated
PO Box 8364, Asheville, NC 28814

Copyright © 2016 Karren LaLonde Alenier
All rights reserved

The Library of Congress has assigned
this edition a Control Number of
2015917764

ISBN 978-1-941196-25-0 (paperback)

Cover art and design by Marc Vincenz
Book design by MadHat Press

www.MadHat-Press.com

First Printing

*In memory of Kathryn E. King, the friend who said I must go to Tangier and meet Paul Bowles.*

## Author's Note

For Paul Bowles, the voice and music are where, if anyplace, he came near the feeling of love. Because of the control his father exacted over him, Bowles made considerable effort to mask his feelings, but his letters, interviews, art songs, and my personal contact with him indicate that he had deep feelings for the female voice, which I equate first to his mother and then later to his wife Jane. I imagine that Gertrude Stein's voice also played into his approach to love. When Jane died, he was completely unmoored. He felt empty. He lived through Jane. It was her husky voice and her unpredictable ways that set him on fire. I have to think this was a form of love and not mere sexual desire.

He was so compromised in feelings that Bruce Morrissette, his best friend when they were both in their late teens, said Bowles was "basically antisexual." Virgil Thomson in a similar vein said, "Paul had a very low sex drive." Intellectually, Paul could say he loved Jane like no other because maybe the truth was that he didn't know if he had ever experienced to his satisfaction what that feeling of love might be. On the other hand, he had deep feelings for her. He said in a 1990 interview with Spanish journalist Soledad Alameda that love was an abstraction and he didn't know what love was. What is clear in reading his letters is that in the spoken and written word and in musical composition were occasions where he came alive. Jane helped him regain the written word after Stein made him doubt himself.

—KLA

## Table of Contents

| | |
|---|---|
| *Author's Note* | vii |
| From the Well, | 1 |

### Section I: In the Secret Club

| | |
|---|---|
| Terrorists | 5 |
| Why a Boy Chooses the University of Virginia | 6 |
| The Sound of It | 8 |
| A College Boy Travels South with Baggage | 9 |
| Yanked | 10 |
| Ether: A College Boy Experiments | 11 |
| Control | 12 |
| Sacrifice: Portrait of a College Boy | 13 |
| Down | 14 |
| Monsters | 15 |
| Between Female and Male | 16 |
| A College Boy Finds His Way | 17 |
| Before This Space Traveler Could Settle | 18 |
| Paris in the Twenties: 1929 | 20 |
| Stories: On the Nature of Poetry | 22 |

### Section II: A Ship Leaving Port

| | |
|---|---|
| Raconteurs in Tangier | 27 |
| Incisor: Cherifa Speaks | 29 |
| When Jane Met Paul, Inimical, She Said | 31 |

| | |
|---|---|
| Hidden Messages: Paul Bowles Introduces Jane Auer to His Family | 32 |
| When You Crossed the Line | 34 |
| Off Course: Bernstein on Bowles | 35 |
| The Parrot That Spoke to Jane Bowles | 36 |
| Epiphany, Years Later: Jane Bowles Reminisces | 37 |
| Riff on "A Quarreling Pair" | 39 |
| Launch | 40 |
| The Recurring Dream of Paul Bowles | 42 |
| Flower: Paul's Love Song | 45 |
| 1934, Jane Bowles Meets Céline | 47 |
| Birth of a Novel | 49 |

## SECTION III: CHASING THE FOX

| | |
|---|---|
| The World Situation | 53 |
| Chasing the Fox: Jane Bowles Visits Her Injury | 54 |
| What Holds | 55 |
| At Sea 1932 | 56 |
| Tongue-Tied Tea, 1960 | 57 |
| Here, Kitty | 59 |
| Edge: Jane's Plaint | 60 |
| No Accident | 62 |
| Bupple's Cat | 63 |
| Gift | 64 |

| | |
|---|---|
| Agonizer | 65 |
| Drawing Room Comedy | 67 |
| On the Beats: Paul Bowles Pushes Back | 71 |
| Strokes | 72 |
| An Onlooker Gossips | 74 |
| They Don't Like Bury Jews in Spain | 75 |
| Hard to Resist | 76 |

### Afterword

| | |
|---|---|
| Exit Interview | 79 |
| | |
| *End Notes* | 80 |
| *Acknowledgments* | 81 |
| *About the Author* | 84 |

*The Anima of Paul Bowles*

# From the Well,

                    I call.
It is my breath traveling
from within: diaphragm,
throat, lips.
                What is dark
looking for light: Mama.

Our beginning,
                a well,
pit of the gut, female
holding: womb. Like ghosts
of sisters and brothers before
me, I hear you practicing
my name, summoning.
I believe
           your voice
love.

# I. IN THE SECRET CLUB

# Terrorists

> "*Tod heil*, my sweet. Wait until the day
> When time's paralysis overtakes this house"
> —Paul Bowles

At eight, I could write in code
faster than I could interpret

my scribbling. What secrets
did I guard? I think of entering

the quiet house. My mother
hiding under my bed.

My mother who read
"The Pit and the Pendulum"

to me. The grandfather
clock in the darkened

hallway ticking
like a metronome

or an angry boy
ready to explode.

*Karren L. Alenier*

# WHY A BOY CHOOSES THE UNIVERSITY OF VIRGINIA

The prisoner—who was that man
thrust into deep darkness—knew
everything I knew: no Inquisition, no
pit, no pendulum could stop someone
like me or him. Right to the brink
of the pit, no light to guide him I
wanted to escape patriarchal rule
even if he—well, what could he do
except tempt rats to gnaw the tight
straps holding him under the swing
of a sharp pendulum; that blade
would part his body in two at
the heart; he had so little time, so
he dipped his fingers in the juice
of the meat—the jailers kept
supplying him—rubbed fragrant
digits over the straps so rats
would chew away his bonds,
while I implored my mother
before Daddy could question
me—send me south to the Mecca
where my master Poe studied Latin,
Greek, French, Spanish, Italian,
where Edgar Allan Poe wrote
"Tamerlane," about a man
eventually tangled in love's hair,
UVA where the poet starved as he
painted his dormitory walls

with nightmare art, his room
number thirteen not far
from Monticello and the aging
author of American independence.

*Karren L. Alenier*

# The Sound of It

"Donnez-moi ce livre
là-bas." So from the floor
the boy picked up a book
that had slid from the old

man's pile. "Here it is,
Daddypapa." "En français,"
the grandfather coaxed.
"Oui!" The boy felt the word

breeze from his small wet
lips. He loved the secret
code of musical sounds
that his grimacing father

did not know. His daddy's
daddy learning a new way
to talk, teaching a willing
protégé. Daddypapa, the

imposing master who made
his son trade violin and bow
for a whining dental drill.

*The Anima of Paul Bowles*

# A College Boy Travels South wth Baggage

1927 New York to Charlottesville Virginia

OK so I was always a mama's
boy but no fit I could employ
would dissuade her from taking
the trip to Charlottesville. If the
choice was Father or Mother, she
would be my pick on the train south
watching the mouth of another boy's
mammy in the hotel lobby asking
about our *V'ginia* lineage.
                                               To hear
the white magnolias wither in that
woman's voice when my ma'am
said, "North, my husband's family
hails from a distant commonwealth—
Massachusetts, not Virginia,"
                                                   "I see,"
the woman said quickly, dropping
her flowery drawl as if Lee lost
the Civil War only yesterday.

*Karren L. Alenier*

# Yanked

|||
|--:|:--|
| born breech | his mother's mother said Paul was |
| yanked by forceps | yanked by Father |
| into the light | out of his crib |
| the infant Paul Bowles | stripped |
| skin orange but | naked |
| mottled with yellow | on a winter's night |
| was saved | plunked into a basket |
| from nuns | the father Pharaoh, the child Moses |
| who wanted | the window flung |
| to baptize him | open |
| his mother | a blizzard |
| a secret Jew | raging |
| threatened | the baby unable |
| to crawl | to do anything except |
| behind them | float, kick, cry |
| screaming | then Grandmother |
| if these black-habited | savior |
| women doused | rescued and covered |
| her son | her posterity |

*The Anima of Paul Bowles*

# Ether: A College Boy Experiments
## Charlottesville Virginia 1928

Under the suffocating cover,
lid off, it hit me—kicked hard
like Poe's "Premature Burial"
watch out for the debris—esker,
kame, terminal moraine, a genie
in small bottle. Ice flames scorch
my throat, numb my limbs where is
my foot, how many quakes of earth—
what did that Italian in 1627 measure—
the intensity of ground shaking—discovering
my mouth corners all down cheeks jelly and
blue while tunes of *Petrouchka* trample my heart
wild its tom-tom beating for the girl with the sweet
sticky lips I'm sliding from my mother's canal now I
am you or the narrator stuck on a sloop in the James how
far to a safe house how far to Richmond the odor of topsoil
telling me I'm Jesus entombed. Help! but only a Negro maid
banging my boarding house door loudly rattling the brass knob
hears my putrid *he he he he.*

Karren L. Alenier

# Control

First I locked
the door so my pen
would not skid
across the page
when he lunged
for it later as I
knew he would.

Picture an eight-year old drawing
houses before breakfast, before
the head of the boy's home
bellowed, *what are you doing
in there?*

When I flipped
the bolt, he pushed
into my room as if
my bed were on fire.
*Well?* He fumed. *Just
drawing*, I shrugged,
*something I thought
you wouldn't like.*

See how this man used his hands—
as a child to hold the body of a violin,
the butt-end of a slender bow. See how
this man used his hands—as a
professional to direct a scalpel
into the gum of an impacted tooth. See
how this man used his hands to bend
the willful child over his knee, crying,
*Had enough?* And when his son clamped
his lips shut, refused to wail—no, he was
silent—the man held out his smarting
hand and grabbed all the offending
notebooks.

## SACRIFICE: PORTRAIT OF A COLLEGE ARTIST
CHARLOTTESVILLE VIRGINIA 1928

The naked body does not live
in my paintings—the dark hair
on private parts, the layers
of flesh, how disgusting those
human models at the New York
School of Design. I resigned myself
to the Worm in D: *Worm in Danger,
Worm in Delight, in Disillusionment,
Damnation, Distress, Disgrace, Decay,
in Dreams, in Detroit, Worm in Death*
—ten abstracts in oil that spoke to my
view of life.
                    Here at UVA, I paint behind
closed doors while my boarding house-
mates shout, "Come out. Are you playing
with yourself?" In every class, there are
those who wear jodhpurs and boots, bring
dogs and guns, sip from hip flasks when
the professors turn their backs. I know
the geology for where to find moonshine
on rocky backroads. It's a provinciality
that gives me social currency. Otherwise
I sold to a student down the hall my black
and white painting called "Sacrifice."

Karren L. Alenier

# Down

> "I am the spider in your salad,
> the bloodsmear on your bread"
>     from "Next to Nothing" by Paul Bowles

The boy I hung
by his feet over the stairwell
from the third floor of my house
as if he were a pendulum
with teeth— "don't drop
me," he chattered, molars
clacking in fear.
            Though the other
boys held the rope with me, he weighed
more than we could hold that cry-
baby blubbering but still wanting
to join the secret club I invented
just to torment him.
            Except for his loud-
mouthed yowling that summoned
my parents and their card-playing
friends into the foyer, his soft thud
exacted no harm.
            In the school yard
first time I saw him, I knew I would torture
him—just like that bully who bloodied
my nose and who Daddymama,
smoothing her coarse gray hair and
pushing me out the door, demanded
I fight till he fell all the way
down.

# Monsters

It's sporting rare to find a monster
like Dracula, the Transylvanian count,
on a small-town stage as featured player.

A tennis star replaced Bela Lugosi as bloodsucker,
but a New York boy at UVA thought it paramount
to hitchhike in 1928 to Lynchburg to find this monster.

"William Tilden was hammy," sniffed the youngster,
"and the scripture-reading locals could not discount
their love for a sappy vampire as featured player."

Next at a Richmond show, the student authored
a plan to vex the vulgar populace—his judgment:
it's sporting rare to find a true monster

sitting as operagoer who uncaps a vial of ether
to inflict a Yankee dodge however tantamount
to a small-town prank by a sophomoric player.

Many fled their seats and *Siegfried* by Wagner.
The boy clapped as Fafnir bore the brunt
of Siegfried's sword finding such a monster
on a hicksville stage as featured player.

*Karren L. Alenier*

## Between Female and Male

The adolescent boy, certainly
thirteen but not much more,
studied a pair of mice, noticed
a difference between the female
and male. Excited he summoned
the biology teacher, "Miss Vickers,
are humans all like this?" His finger
hovered over the tail ends of the two
pinned creatures now dead on their backs.
His classmates snickered and clapped
hands over their mouths. The teacher,
big-busted and heavy-set—no student
wanted to tangle with her quick ruler,
snorted and snapped, "That's enough
out of you, Paul Frederick Bowles."

# A College Boy Finds His Way
## 1929: Charlottesville, New York, Paris

On his 18th birthday, he flipped
a coin but in truth he said he medi-
tated on a curvy
                bottle of sleeping
pills. Time passed. He couldn't pic-
ture being dead so
                Heads!—he fled
to Paris, high-tailed it first to New
York without beloved
                books and records
to collect a passport, slept with bed
bugs in a seedy hotel, didn't bother
to tell his mother or his best friend
in Richmond. There was nothing
to learn at UVA except the way
of the good ole boys
                was not his.

*Karren L. Alenier*

## BEFORE THIS SPACE TRAVELER COULD SETTLE

When the envelope came—
brown, the return reading
*Paris France* my name
*Paul Frederick Bowles*
prominently scripted
as addressee a magazine
couched inside—surprise:
my name on the cover
in the company of
André Breton,
James Joyce,
Gertrude Stein
just to name a few,
the elite avant-garde,
my poem "Spire Song"
in six parts there in
*transition* with the best.
My feet left the floor.
I leaped, no law of gravity
could limit my joy. I hollered
and before this space traveler
could settle again on natal ground
I had written a prophecy: *P. F. Bowles,
degrees from every American college,
appointed poet laureate in the royal
court of King Edward.* Why? Because
I swam the Atlantic under water,

emerged triumphant and wet on British
soil where I recited my poem unfaltering
in a loud and sonorous voice.

*Karren L. Alenier*

## Paris in the Twenties: 1929

I.

Manhattan ferry
to Hoboken—the day before
Easter, 40 degrees Fahrenheit, cold
breeze, Fifth Street pier, the Rijndam
waited. In his pocket not much
cash but three letters of introduction.
                              Just eight
Paris-bound passengers.
He read *Le Journal des Faux-
Monnayeurs*, that book about a boy, 16,
leaving home, adrift in the streets of Paris.
Christine, wife of a count, belly full
of child, taught the runaway French
street slang. Gide taught the prodigal
the struggle to write, the blend of dream,
missteps, disappointments, joy—no,
*elation* when the right word resurrects
the page.

II.

How does one write
explain as Gide did
to his journal the incident
of the real life boy stealing
a book in Gide's novel within
a novel filled with good and bad
pedophiles, married women and men
who cheat? Does one take this to the
streets of Paris or the bed of nettles

*The Anima of Paul Bowles*

where the college boy lost his virginity
first to a woman and later to a so-called
cousin—that man who brought money
from the runaway's father to Paris at the end
of the Twenties, already losing its effervescent
spark.

Karren L. Alenier

## Stories: On the Nature of Poetry

If I Paul Frederick Bowles tell you
Gertrude Stein wrote to my mother
to say Rena's son Freddy—that's what the great
Buddha called me—was a self-indulgent savage
who augured the end of civilization
and Mother cheerfully sent "poor old
Sophie and Alice B. Luckless"
family recipes...

If I tell you
the Mama of Dada dressed me
in lederhosen so her great white
poodle Basket, wet from his daily
sulphur bath—the French countryside
vermin otherwise crawling into the dog's
curls to suck his skin red—could chase
me and scrape his sharp long nails
into my bare legs while his master
shouted from the second story
window, "Faster, Freddy, faster..."

If I tell you
*transition*—a Paris magazine
that published Ezra Pound—printed
"Spire Song" by Paul Frederick Bowles...
I was only seventeen. When I was twenty,
the iconic Miss Stein said, "Freddy,
you don't write great poetry." I believed
her and left the City of Light
for the filth of Tangier.

*The Anima of Paul Bowles*

If I tell you I traded the truth
of poetry for the invention
of prose. If I tell you I lived
loving a wife who filled
my dry pen while hers
spurted blood
like a shotgun wound.
If I tell you my stories,
greater than the lives
of people I knew ...
if I tell you my stories,
how many times
would you say I lied?

## II. A Ship Leaving Port

*The Anima of Paul Bowles*

# RACONTEURS IN TANGIER

> "What can go wrong is always more
> interesting *than what goes right.*"
> —Paul Bowles

Cherifa, tell me those stories
about you as shadow
of Jane Bowles, breathing
on her neck, shining light
into her mouth, the pain
she suffered, waves
of pain from a bad
tooth—too much sugar
in her mint tea. Ha! Like me,
you suspected the *majoun*
sticky with raisins, dates,
honey, ground ginger,
walnuts, nutmeg, anise,
globs of goat butter
and of course cannabis,
cleaned of stems
and seeds.
              You profited
as her dentist in Tangier. No!
You played would-be
biographer trying to extract
details about her wedding,
her marriage to me, Paul Bowles.
Persistent, you declared yourself
devotée, lived with her, wore
her clothes but never noticed

*Karren L. Alenier*

she called her husband *Bupple*
or *Fluffy*—look at me, that man
answering his door in necktie
and jacket, that man who named
her *his* muse.
                But she limped,
didn't she? She lived on a floor below
me. You probably wonder if I chose
a Jew to embarrass my father. You ate
with us the night I ranted about
my family. Do you think Jane served
as my cover, that my mother expected
grandchildren? The simple truth
is I loved her as I loved no other.
Tell me, was it true her female
lovers like you poisoned her?

# Incisor: Cherifa Speaks

*I smoke with my dead lover's
husband because his kif
tastes good.*

                  Paul talks about a snake
and the body of a boy who lost
his mind to this slithering
creature. He forgets even women
like me can hear this story
in the souk.
              Behind that screen
of smoke, his eyes burn
like coals.
          He blames me, Cherifa,
descendent of the Patron Saint
of Tangier, for the death
of his wife Jane.
               What kind of marriage
between these two? I knew her better,
inside and out, than this hungry-looking
liar who says he grieves.

When he journeyed to Ceylon, I took Jane
to my dentist. She bought me this gold
tooth. "A voluptuous woman should care
for her teeth," Jane said to me.
                  That torturer,
he yanked out my incisor—a rotten
tooth I howled over like a moon struck
dog. Jane swore I could be her dentist

before she let that butcher
touch her.
     She hated doctors. They crippled
her knee. Sometimes she screamed
she wanted to be a python to crush
those who stood
in her way.
     When did Mr. Bowles hold Jane
in his spidery arms? She gave me his den
in the Casbah. The two of us could crawl
in there and drink until my name was hers
and hers mine. She feared *majoun*,
said it would seal her mouth
like cement.
     Has the master forgotten
how greedy Jane became the first time
she tasted that dark candy?
     Story-
tellers invent their own truths,
trafficking in gossip that twists
people's heads. Last night in a dark
alley, I heard him say, "Cherifa
laughs like a savage."
     No, I laugh
like the wild canine I am. I spit
on Paul's shoes. What
does he know? An American,
he thinks that spit is for shine.

*The Anima of Paul Bowles*

# WHEN JANE MET PAUL, *INIMICAL*, SHE SAID

blond but not
*amicus* as in
*curiae* not
friend of my court
but courtly
no *ami* but
cuss
persistent
not exactly
gadfly more
mysterious
more dangerous
is he fair,
this composer
poseur—the eyes
don't lie
do I like him?
do I? what if I sit
in his lap? what if
I let him touch
my hand? what
if, what if I stick
my tongue out.
I say Paul Bowles
my enemy.

*Karren L. Alenier*

# Hidden Messages
## Paul Bowles Introduces Jane Auer to His Family

Chapter 1

                     In French on their first
bus ride south to Mexico, Paul whispered to Jane
about the family tradition on his mother's side:
with hammers, fathers smashing their sons' noses
making the bridge flat. All of them became
atheists. "Sensuality and religion," Paul leaned close
but did not touch, "two things my father did not tolerate.
Mother held her tongue—she feared her husband. My
grandparents thought they raised
a Christian son."
                    Wearing Paul's fedora and igniting
a short Cuban cigar, Jane, a Jew who didn't know how
to be Jewish, laughed but touched her stiffened
knee. She scribbled in a notebook, "and certain people
won't leave God alone either."
                            Paul studied his left
hand, remembered out loud how his father struck
that hand, the dominant hand, forcing
him to use the right.
                   "I was always hungry, Jane. If I asked
for seconds, my father said *no, you must learn to chew
each morsel forty times.*" Paul, blue-eyed, blond, already
pale, blanched and lowered his voice more, "I threw
a meat cleaver at that man."

Chapter 2

           Jane circled her pen over the white space,
then wrote, "There are certain people who turn peace

from the door as though it were a red dragon breathing
fire out its nostrils." She wrinkled her pug nose, narrowed
her brown eyes at Paul, same face as when her mother shoved
several evening gowns with matching shoes into her suitcase,
telling her, "Of course, you will stay
at the Ritz Mexico City."
    Paul opened his pack, showed her
15,000 stickers screaming in red letters for the death
of Trotsky. "I'm thinking of joining the Communist
Party."

Months later meeting Rena, Paul's mother, Jane said,
"You double Fanny Kaplan, the Jewess who tried
to assassinate Lenin." Jane made a mental note,
*two serious ladies in a quandary*
*about what to say.*

## Chapter 3

    After they left Rena with her jaw hanging, Jane wanted
to play I Forgive You For All Your Sins. "Let me pack
you in mud," Jane said gleefully, "and dunk you in your tub."
But Paul had another family story—Leonard Bernstein called
Rena *a nice Jewish lady* to which Paul, indignant,
retorted, "She's not."
    "Get out! Who are you kidding?"
Then Lenny demanded to see the family photos. "There,"
he tapped his finger on the glass protecting
Rena's brother—"*yeshiva bucher*, a Chosen One,
learned and starving."

*Karren L. Alenier*

# When You Crossed the Line

to Mexico, your girlfriend wouldn't get off
the bus. In the back row, Jane crouched
at the feet of Indian women. She cowered
among their babies, their sacks of dried
beans. Years later and oceans away,
she told me—Cherifa, her toothsome
Moroccan love of her life—everything
scared her—the yapping dogs
in the dusty streets, the drunken
bus driver, the rise and fall
of the land.	In Mexico City, she fled
to the Ritz just like her mama insisted.
Then you found her, flat in bed, losing
all her fluids, surrounded by flowers
she bought for herself. Sick as she
was, you made a foolish lunch date
for the next day, but she ran, flew
to Tucson where she met a carnival
freak—a woman half man or a man half
woman. She said Navajos called
this queer *nadle*, considered this mis-
fit a blessing.	Paul Bowles, your lover left
you for a nadle, flirted with this fright
over dinner.

## OFF COURSE: BERNSTEIN ON BOWLES

Marriage, a strange pipe dream Jane and Paul culled
from scenarios rife with randy things
bound to jolt their parents and good friends too.

No shock to Lenny B, I know how bold
how bent my friend Paul on juvenile flings.
I mean his Christian father with a Jew—

Jane, gimpy kike dyke—as daughter-in-law!
Paul, such a Romeo! Oh! I hear strings.
Queer bait Paul, sea legs Jane—too much to chew.

To be first mate, catch them swear as ship yaws
                    I do.

*Karren L. Alenier*

# The Parrot that Spoke to Jane Bowles

*Budupple, budupple-mah, rop*
the parrot said to Jane. Not,
*Hi, where is your money?* Not, *Hello,*
*take me home!*
　　　　　　　　After the sunrise horse-
back ride—clip clop—with fifteen cowboys
through the Costa Rican jungle, trees laden
with howler monkeys, the big black male
roaring, swinging from his tail, tiny
babies clinging to their mother's
teats, Jane and Paul were offered one
of seven young parrots.
　　　　　　　　"Nonsense," Jane squawked,
"I don't break up families."
　　　　　　　　But Budupple perched alone
on a man's fingers, so they bagged him in a burlap
sugar sack, along with their 27 trunks
and Paul's typewriter.
　　　　　　　　Jane heard him say, *Don't pinch me*
but Paul retorted, *He'll never learn English.* The parrot ate
their peppermint toothpaste, one Russian
novel, and Jane's tortoise-shell
lorgnette much to her delight—
that gift from her mother,
she never liked it anyhow.

# Epiphany, Years Later
## Jane Bowles Reminisces

> "When my tongue blabs,
> then let mine eyes not see."
> *Twelfth Night*, William Shakespeare

Helvetia, Velveeta, big
cheese, one Swiss
hunk of a lover, twice
my twenty-three years
when I spied her walking
the streets of Taxco.
                    "Boo,"
I had said to you, my drinking
partner, "Boo Bob, I'm going
to spin her head. *If music
be the food of love*, I'll give
her an excess of my voice.
*La, la.* Janie's not married
to a prominent composer
for nothing. Aren't
Helvetia's eyes painfully
blue? Aren't her eyes ice-
cracking blue? If I were Queen
of the Bean, she would obey
only me. How long can she sit
at her desk with her back turned
when I want to eat cake? Would
that I were a slender pen in her
hand."
        Look at us, Boo, still bending

our elbows, drinking without memory
of dawn cracking up the black
sky over Manhattan. I tremble
with fear because in my cramped
big city room, my novel taps its toe
like an angry wife.
     Boo, when
we left my shoes and Helvetia behind—
a train trip out of Mexico in sandals,
headed in December to New York and Paul,
Paul writing incidental music for *Twelfth Night*
while I wrote not even a card—you,
Mister Boo, played Mother, bought
me boots and stockings all lost
in some depot along the way.
       Helvetia's
daughter, thought me witty but mean,
that my tongue carved innocents
to bits.
   Hey, Boo, but my words were no sharper
than the blade I took to my wrists years later
at the Bowles country estate. There,
Helvetia kept writing—me, I could only
bleed.

# RIFF ON "A QUARRELING PAIR"
## (A PUPPET PLAY BY JANE BOWLES)

Two sisters sans misters
fight over evening milk.

Sad, big-hearted younger
considers leaving home.

Cold, orderly elder
quakes at being alone.

The neater offers a glass;
the sloppy slams with a crash.

No mother serves tea—
spilled, both cups empty.

One shouts *game*;
other, sings blame.

Two Judys
punch the void.

*Karren L. Alenier*

## Launch

> "If a woman is not pregnant,
> never anticipates live children,
> she still expects to procreate."

Her mother Claire, her Aunt Birdie,
even her lover Helvetia who bore
that sassy daughter Nora expected

Janie to produce. And what exactly
did Jane Bowles mean shouting
in gaming glee to Paul, "you've ruined

my uterus." In the Brooklyn brownstone
where Jane typed Auden's words and hung
on his theory that Kafka's every story

worried: *God has forsaken us*, Paul nagged
Jane to police her own work. He scrapped
with the acclaimed poet over Kafka,

"Man into insect only astonishes.
Forget religion." Jane cut Paul off,
"Get back in your cage, Bupple."

Not until they left New York
and returned to Taxco did Jane—
alternating between scratching out

words just written, anguishing
over the affair with Helvetia
and always the drinking,

the partying—did Jane finally deliver
*Two Serious Ladies* to Paul, proud
papa, but he shouted at his wife

for the mess of spelling, the faulty
punctuation. "Gloompot, if a publisher
likes my baby, his editor will groom

my book." Thoughtfully Paul rejoined
by quoting Jane's Mr. Copperfield,
a character even Aunt Birdie thought

was Paul himself, "For god's sake,
a ship leaving port is still
a wonderful thing to see."

*Karren L. Alenier*

## The Recurring Dream of Paul Bowles

Inside the cage of night
when I fall in fitful
sleep, the erotic one strides

toward me wrapped
in a white sheet,
head bald like a cancer

patient or an orthodox
Jew in her boudoir. "Anaïs,"
I whisper, "what bed

at Middaugh House
did you strip? Wystan
Auden's? Benjamin

Britten and Peter Pears'?
Klaus Mann's? Mine
on the third floor?

Mr. Auden, housemother
during that year before
Pearl Harbor when

we writers and composers
lived and wrote in that
Brooklyn brownstone,

*The Anima of Paul Bowles*

would have shook
his moral finger, "How dare
you steal our dirty linens!"

but Jane, your target,
received that endless
letter—eight primly typed

pages outlining
the faults of *Two
Serious Ladies*.

In a snowstorm, you
ambushed Jane
on Eighth Street.

"One sheet for every
street," I muttered,
holding a huge load

of groceries. Forty
minutes, hoping
the bag would not

dissolve in the heavy,
cold downfall! And yet
Jane laughed after

*Karren L. Alenier*

you left us and said
years later, "What could
Henry Miller's bitch,

and a bigamist to boot,
what could the erotic
Anaïs Nin know

about my religion,
the many ways
I have failed?"

## FLOWER: PAUL'S LOVE SONG

Because the hotel manager floated
scores of our favorite flower on the surface
of the swimming pool, Jane and I decided
to visit the Taxco market and buy enough
gardenias to cover our bed.
                            At siesta careful
not to arouse staff sleepyheads, we carried two
baskets of blossoms in several trips
into the hotel and up the stairs. When the bed
became a sea of creamy white, we undressed,
lay down and drowned our senses.

How much is too much?

In the blue fluid of the pool Jane Bowles poked
her head, short curly hair winking red,
through the fragrant corollas — a swoon
of flower boats.
                  Could a husband and wife, sheath
and knife, be joined in everlasting memory
on a perfumed spread of gardenias? She
with her women; me, Paul Bowles,
with my men.

Could I recreate those hours we lay
together?

In New York I furnished everything in white:
sofa, chaise longue, Ottoman, coffee table,
lamps, a polar bear rug. Then I sprayed

Karren L. Alenier

the drapes, and every pillow, every throw
with ambergris mixed with crushed
petals of gardenia.
*Come back
from Taxco*, I wrote to her.

What price paradise?

*The Anima of Paul Bowles*

# 1934, Jane Bowles Meets Céline

### With comments from Paul

after the TB
          after I learned
of the knee
          how intimate she
cure two years locked
          with Bardamu
in Dr. Rollier's rack—
          Céline's alter
bones and flesh pulled
          ego the horse-
in opposite directions—
          man wounded
my mother Claire and I crossed
          WWI NCO
*Voyage au bout*
          later poor-
*de la nuit* in hand
          man's doc
my Swiss tutors fed me
          she floored
Gide, Proust, Céline *le fou*
          me with her story
*au coeur et puis au cul* how well
          16 years old on the
I could swear in French then he said
          Champlain manifest
I see you're reading
          meeting the one writer

*Karren L. Alenier*

Céline I said one
              I Paul Bowles
of the greatest he said
              avoided for
Céline *c'est moi*
              five decades

# Birth of a Novel
## Paul Bowles Confesses

The sky was not sheltering
in the desert even a rock
could mean a little more life

from the incendiary sun
my mentor should I call him
that once said work when

you are 20 nobody will love
you at 30 nearly 40 when
my art switched hands

from music to words
came the reviews
I traveled from the light

of music to the merciless
shade of stories that would
redeem me but not my characters.

# III. Chasing the Fox

*The Anima of Paul Bowles*

# The World Situation

As the wife fed her cat crab-
meat, the cat that attempted
to walk the ceiling but failed,
the husband tackled the decline
of American civilization—barbarians
populated his tales. If a man cried
out, another lopped off his tongue.
In private, she said TV and
McCarthyism killed the invention
of new games. He just ripped
the caterwauling telephone
from the wall.
          At a dinner party of all
women except for him, when she
was asked to comment on the world
situation, she excused herself, left
what was tasty and steaming
on the table, curled regally
on a divan like a feline, fell
asleep under an open
window.
          With its slow white
flakes, snow covered her. Horrified
at her absence, weren't these women
her friends, he shook her awake—
*what game is this?* She whispered,
*Resistance To Doom. I had to
make room for hope.*

*Karren L. Alenier*

# CHASING THE FOX:
## JANE BOWLES VISITS HER INJURY

My mother Claire wore fox
fur and Shalimar perfume
for my Stoneleigh boarding
school interview. She sat up
straight, patted my thigh,
"You see my daughter is
special," Eyes narrowing
and nostrils glistening,
the headmistress unfurled
her rolled handkerchief
and leaned close
to hear Claire say,
"Jane is a Jewess."
                        The agony
I felt riding the pedestal Claire built
for a princess. When I fell from my mount,
the horse, whiter than a WASP in winter,
looked as surprised as the little girl
dusting off her habit and clutching
her throbbing knee.
                      As for the fox,
red as fever, she winked at the dogs
that had lost her scent. Woof! I barked
when I should have howled.

## What Holds

When my mother Claire isn't hovering, she's scanning the Champlain for men. If Daddy were alive, he'd say, "Now, Claire, let Jane find her way." Hmph, transatlantic crossing notwithstanding, I can barely stand after two years in the Alps—a sick ward wretch. And where was Claire—in Paris drinking good wines and handling the goods of the best shops. She prides herself on matching shoes and handbags, seeking tiny stitches holding together the seams of kid gloves. What holds me together against everything I fear is a book like this one, *Voyage au bout de la nuit*. Céline, now there's a writer who does not hold back.

*Karren L. Alenier*

## At Sea 1932

Jane Auer Meets Louis-Ferdinand Céline

Who is that man touching the cover of my daughter's book, the one we bought in Paris after I took her from the clinic in Switzerland? Her knee, now purged of TB, still causes great pain but the novel, darker than these nights at sea, ambush the hurt better than the pills Dr. Rollier prescribed. Look at that man, so much older than my Janie, only seventeen, but he's handsome, maybe forty and goodness! Jane is smiling, releasing the book and her pen to his hand.

# Tongue-Tied Tea, 1950

Sitting there. Waiting to hear
something intelligent, Alice offers
me a steaming cup.
     Could I tell her
Eudora Welty failed to read "Camp
Cataract?" Eudora sent it back
to me in the mail, asking
for a different story.
     What
could be more different, a story
about sisters who try to escape
each other until finally the one
no one would suspect separates
her body from theirs?
     I can't converse
so I consume the multi-colored bread
stuffed with savory fillings.
     "Jane Bowles," Alice
Toklas scolds, "you like the sandwiches better
than my cakes."
     She speaks the truth
and I want to hide just like a child
ordered to open wide on the first
visit to a dentist.
     Like those suicidal fingers
of confection arranged on Alice's antique
plates, I line them up—none of them sweet—
Harriet, Sadie, Evy and even Beryl who dreams
union as their sister. On a fresh slate, I parade
each one to the cataract to understand how

*Karren L. Alenier*

water cascading over rocks can heal. I line
them up but sacrifice the sister
in the middle once
again.

# Here, Kitty

Come, my sharp-clawed cat,
linger by my pillow. I'll chase

sleep's flight into darkness.
There, I can touch the latch

of your years, that long fur
embedded deep in the skin.

If I hold my hand out, your razor
tongue might taste the aquatics

I swallowed whole. How many
oysters must slide down

my throat before you mark
me. My heart ticks wildly

like that old wall clock
loaded with a crazed

bird. Here, my tightly knotted
carpet, my gate to the gut,

nine lives in one, I cut myself
wide open for you.

Karren L. Alenier

## EDGE: JANE'S PLAINT

If I could live
in her world, penetrate
her culture, speak

her language, ululate
with her sisters—Jews
and Arabs, aren't we sparked

and spanked from the same,
the same daddy, Oh! Abraham,
lying with Sarah, lying

with Hagar—the desert
sand sifts into my bed.
No, maybe it's her

grain, those mountains
of barley, wheat, oats,
her shining black

eyes and hair, her
laughter in the market
wilder than a hyena

alerting her clan,
*Come quick I'll guard
the feast for the family—*

*The Anima of Paul Bowles*

that could be me running
toward her, tight in the hungry
herd. Me without limp

to retard my progress.
I know the tasty morsel
could be me: her gobbling

my flesh, bones, nails, hair,
leaving my parts in pellets
far from her cave. If I could live

in her world, reach that edge,
my own darkness, the abyss
would liberate me from fear.

*Karren L. Alenier*

# No Accident

About the time a djinn grabbed
hold of the leather-bound steering
wheel and our driver who warned
days before of the hovering demon
crashed my husband's Jaguar
into a stone bridge, I turned the dusty
pages of my calendar to discover
I had become by no accident
thirty-five.          To breathe now or die,
always my battle cry against the clock
that killed my heart-weak daddy, I let
my friends be my mirror—I had no
child except myself. Was my hair
fashionably combed? My red-as-blood
lipstick on straight? Did my right shoe
show wear from my stiff-legged
limp?          I caught myself mid-syllable
talking in the same frantic
cadence as  my mother. I could
mimic anyone but feared glimpsing
even her eyes in any windowpane
but, oh, to hear her voice in mine, far
worse than the tire screech
and the too-late brakes.

## Bupple's Cat

Yes, Tennessee, I know about Bupple's cat
on a hot tin roof that crazy-legged
girl he once knew—she Charlestoned on the edge—
the parapet of the Central Park South. How
many stories up—30? 32? 34?—
from the glittering sidewalk below people
hurried home from work or dragged
their feet not wanting to turn knobs
leading to conflict.
               Humph but did she ever rescue
a sheet of music that blew from Paul's hand? His Janie crawled
out on that rooftop ledge over Tenth Street to grab it while Paul froze
watching me.
               Paul Bowles told me he could not sleep could not eat
that that daughter of a lesbian, daughter of a rake could make trips
to men's toilets just to read the graffiti on the walls. A beautiful
boy she could be. She was expelled from every school in the City,
every academy in London.
             And yes, Tennessee, he lent her everything:
books records money, talked hours on the phone blowing her
kisses, laughing as she teased him and still he called her his only
only only.

*Karren L. Alenier*

# Gift

Without fanfare, she said, "Give it to me."
Then the opium vanished in one flush.
Vexed, he asked, "Why couldn't you let it be?"
Their friend the playwright laughed hard and said, "Hush!"

Then Tennessee's drugs vanished in one flush.
"Come with me, Paul, to see our leg our lamb."
Their friend the playwright laughed hard and said, "Hush!"
"Tennessee paid the butcher in dirhams."

"Come with me, Paul, to see our leg our lamb.
Afterwards let's watch the blue people dance.
Tennessee paid the butcher in dirhams."
Fire, earth, water, wind—a blessed trance.

"Afterwards let's watch the blue people dance."
Vexed, Paul asked, "Why couldn't you let it be?"
Fire, earth, water, wind—a blessed trance.
Sans fanfare, Jane said, "He gave it to me."

# Agonizer

Dear Bupple,

I play and replay what I will say in this letter. Not sure what will actually be written—I cannot control my pen and this is likely to be an agonizer. I tell myself not to mention that night in the Chelsea Hotel when you hit me. I said then and meant it, "I forgive you."
    The trouble is I must forgive you again and again for that moment frozen in memory. I know you needed to sleep, so you could write music for Saroyan's *Love's Old Sweet Song*.
    Do you remember our honeymoon—the night in Guatemala City when we met those students in a café? The ones reading Proust and Valéry? How I wanted to stay and talk to them. The beer was so bitter and you, Paul Bowles, so bored. Tired, you fled to our hotel.
    Those pups made me giddy with talk and tequila carried from Mexico. They got the cat out of her bag. I grew so curious. "Have you ever seen a brothel," one rakish guy asked. "No, show me one." So the boys and I left the café for a house at the edge of town.
    Inside the bad-girl door, a huge man dressed in uniform, packing a pistol in a holster on his hip pointed to me, "That one." Who was he? Why me? "I am the chief bodyguard of the dictator of Guatemala," he boasted. Bodyguards surrounded him. Terrified, I thought I would wet myself, but the working girls hustled me to a back room and shoved me out a window.

                              I hid behind a mountain
of stinking garbage. The bodyguards drove the streets
shining a spotlight into every dark corner. How I got
back to you alive, I don't know. I vowed I would never
say what happened. The pen pulls its own tricks.
                                                    Paul, why
couldn't you be civil to Dick the Shit in our New York City
hotel room? He was just drunk, same as me. Just trying
to have fun, same as me. What trouble could there be
in reveling? And that woman in our tub, the one
wearing my peignoir, the gift from my mother—
so what! I would never tell Claire about her. That
woman with unnaturally bright red hair, Claire

would never know that drunken, passed-out
woman wearing the gray silk
gown wasn't me.
                            Claire, I should always call my mother
by her name—*Claire de lune*. How crazy she makes me
still after all these years. Always, Jane

## DRAWING ROOM COMEDY

I.
My husband Paul Bowles bought an island
off the coast of Ceylon.
                Taprobane
had an octagonal house opened
to the elements—no closing
doors or windows, no permanent
interior walls.
             At night, large-tooth bats
with three-foot wing spans, soared
through our lotus hall.
                 Initially, we wasted
our flashlight batteries to gawk
at the beasts—so many of them
in our garden hanging
in the trees.
           At first four of us—
Paul, Paul's protégé Ahmed, our driver
Temsamany and I occupied
the house sleeping in alcoves
made private by curtains. I couldn't sleep,
the heat burned more intense than Panama.

II.
"Timmie," I said, "turn on the light.
In the house of Poe are things that bite."
But in the flicker of the oil lamp, menacing
shadows populated our camp.
                     "Timmie,"
I said, "kill that pungent flame. God

only knows why I came."
                         I couldn't sleep
and there was nothing to drink.

                              "Timmie,"
I said, "turn on the light. My hair is a fright.
It's falling out in clumps. That devil drumming
on the mainland scares me, makes me
jump. Walk on the water, tell them to stop.
My ears are gonna pop! Fit a sunbill
over my twitching eyes, then maybe
I could write till I drop.
                        What deep pit
will I plummet into? What hairy fingers
and stinging tails will grab
and stab me? Timmie, Timmie,
douse that fire. No, no, bring me
whiskey! How about gin?
With this thirst, I could ignite
a funeral pyre."

III.
While every morning at sunrise
Paul, dressed in a sarong, wrote
*The Spider's House*, I, the Spider's
Wife, meditated on a drawing room
comedy. Not a comedy, more a moral
tract about a married pair: she, jealous;
he, indifferent; each enjoying many
suitors.

*The Anima of Paul Bowles*

    Ahmed Yacoubi set up his easel
and painted primitive landscapes.
Paul coached, encouraged, breathed
down Ahmed's neck—pretty boy Ahmed,
eyes, black and deep like caves. Ahmed
who plays his flute to blow life
into his finished painting.
                          Timmie dreamed
about Paul's Jaguar, parked and unmanned
in Tangier.

IV.
            But I couldn't think and I had nothing
to drink. Was I a faker bored with the daily rain—
what was wrong with my brain? Did Paul whisper
I was a neurotic sick at the lack of friends to gossip
with at the local pub? Or did I Jane Bowles
swallowing Serpasil, a blood pressure
drug, suffer a damaged heart? Why
couldn't I start my play?
                     I said, "Timmie, let's pick up
our skirts, visit Colombo. Low tide now, we won't get
that wet." Not be dry, that was my plan. Down a few
rounds, kick off my shoes and dance, fly quenched.

V.
Then came Peggy Guggenheim ready to slum
with artists out on the edge. Unlike Libby
Holman hoping to marry Paul and call me
sister, Peggy didn't even bat lashes

at my mister. Peggy, just an heiress
complaining about wetting her bottom
on the low-tide wade to Taprobane—hey!
no gondolas waited at convenient wharves
—the other lacks, no running water
for a shower, no electric lights
to illuminate her bedtime
novel, didn't raise her well-plucked
eyebrows.          Actually, she noticed
my distress, offered to take me
to Bombay and Calcutta, *but India*,
I sniffed, *meant withdrawing
from my work*. My subjects played
on the black basalt of Paul's island.

VI.
So Peggy and I spent a week in Colombo,
circling Ahmed's flat images. I served as her wife.
She wouldn't let me share her bed, but I know
I got into her head. The head that saw
our house on Taprobane
as the Taj Mahal.          But I still couldn't think
and had too much to drink. All the webs
of my dear spider could not cradle,
could not rock, those endless hours
on that tropical clock.

*The Anima of Paul Bowles*

## ON THE BEATS: PAUL BOWLES PUSHES BACK

Beat? Me? Sure
I knew Bill Burroughs. He lived here
in Tangier throwing yellow foolscap
that oversized paper scrawled with
*Naked Lunch* on the filthy floor
those unnumbered pages marked
with heel scuffs, rat droppings,
bits of stinking sardines and moldy
sandwich bread. I couldn't stop
myself, I said, "Why don't you
pick it up?" He just shrugged, peeled
back the wrapper on his candy bar,
and took a bite, "Someday, when the
time is right."

Beat? Me? No
I wasn't in Tangier the year, let's say
1957, when Kerouac and later Ginsberg
with his sidekick Peter O. showed up
at the brothel where Burroughs lived.
They picked up the pages, typed the
illegible words and stacked, then posted
the interchangeable chapters to the
publisher. Voilà, a trifecta of success
*Howl, On the Road, Naked Lunch*
These men like monks wrote together
finishing each other's sentences in
beatific holy bliss—so many deserts
between us.

*Karren L. Alenier*

## Strokes

                    I can't take it
with me so I'm handing
it away—money, pearls,
diamond earrings that made me
sparkle, and my best dresses
and shoes.
                My mother will be horrified—
I can hear Claire's voice now. *Janie
Auer Bowles, the things I gave you?* But, Mother,
those hippies, long-haired girls and boys, snuggle
close, stroke my arm at the Atlas and Parade
bars where I drink and they whisper about love,
peace, and a little Moroccan
reefer.
                If they say give me five, I give them
ten. The bougainvillea they steal from the vines
by the door, I nest in my wacky wig. Only when
I'm stripped bare will I quit and one day I did
just that, entered the Parade nude, nada,
nothing on the fifty-year body that fails
me—fingers, tongue, brain that can't move
my pen. If I could record what these flower
friends tell me, I would stop wringing
my useless hands, stop worrying
that everything I see
I see crooked.
                    For years Alice Toklas sent
emissaries to urge me, *apply ink
to paper: a stroke here, a stroke
there, adds up.*

*The Anima of Paul Bowles*

           Dear Daddy, tell me heart
failure sudden and swift isn't better
than strokes slowing the brain,
making me painful witness
to words I cannot say,
words I cannot write.

*Karren L. Alenier*

## An Onlooker Gossips

Stooge, the philodendron, served
as the Moroccan maid's stand-in
channeling intimate orders that cut
through reason. Magic in a dirty

cloth containing fingernails, pubic
hairs, sticky phlegm, dried blood
buried in the potted plant's loam.
At 52, the mistress still slept

with a stuffed koala bear, dreading
night shadows, dosing and dozing
fitfully. If the hired woman poisoned
the husband's parrot, flashed

the quick blade of her mechanical
knife in his direction, what injury
did she coax her green spy to do
to his little girl muse?

*The Anima of Paul Bowles*

# They Don't Like Burying Jews in Spain

### Jane Bowles (1917–1973)

Paul, even if I cannot speak, I know you can
read my mind. What could be worse than baisar,
that thick pea soup Moroccans eat in rainy

season? People gossip that Cherifa poisoned
your Janie, mixing magic potions into my pea
porridge. You correct them, say, *datura*, locoweed.

Look at me. Not true. Why would I eat that green
mortar? Daddy fell at forty-five—what is hyper-
tension to a kid in camp? *Do you believe in God?*

the bop poet Allen Ginsberg once asked me. Same
question these nuns who care for me here outside
Málaga ask. To them, God and Jesus are one.

Don't fret, Bupple, unlike Alice Toklas coerced
by that Nazi Bernard Faÿ, my conversion
accommodates my keepers. Catholicism,

another thick potage. Take my hand, sign
the release for my religious bath. Let them think
I'm Catholic. Paul, a wink between you and me.

I'll be joining Daddy in The Garden soon.

*Karren L. Alenier*

## Hard to Resist

    Paul Bowles on Jane

Of course she was my kind
of girl, terrorizing her neighbor-
hood—painting the wet laundry
blue, jumping horses at a boarding
school where Janie was the only
                            Jew,
egging me on in my mimicry of
Truman Capote when she was clearly
the master. She said she made sloppy
stews on a hot plate for him in a Paris
hotel room years after I tried to show
                         my bride
to the only woman who could tell me
what to do. *Hello, Alice. Freddie here.*
*Did you receive my petit bleu? I want*
*to introduce my wife Jane to Miss Stein*
*and you.* Summer 1938 not to be—
                        Gertrude
and Alice leaving for the countryside. Soon
the war separating us. Then Jane's novel
making me believe I could pick up the pen
and write words of consequence. She was
my kind of muse: elusive, comically dark,
                      hard to resist.

# Afterword

## Exit Interview

I loved her?
    After
all those years
I don't know
    what
love is—I used to think
it was in my music there
I could say anything feel
anything be reborn out
of the hands of a jealous
man wanting my mother
without competition I
learned this New
England game
    to say
the opposite of what
I desired what I needed
to live now I have nothing
inside she lent me her
womb in that place I could
compose true words I could
leave my body behind.

# End Notes

PAUL BOWLES was born December 30, 1910, and died November 18, 1999. He was a composer, fiction writer, and poet. He grew up in the Jamaica Queens neighborhood of New York City. He married fiction writer and playwright Jane Auer in 1938. She died May 4, 1973 in Malaga, Spain. Bowles settled in Tangier, Morocco in 1947 and made Tangier his home until his death. In the early 1950s, he wintered in Ceylon (now known as Sri Lanka).

Author of four novels, Bowles is best known for *The Sheltering Sky*, which was published in 1949. A prolific story writer, he also translated the work of many writers including Jean Paul Sartre's play *Huis clos* (*No Exit*), a translation that still stands today as the definitive English translation. As a protégé of Aaron Copland, Bowles went on to write operas, incidental music for films and plays including those of Tennessee Williams, and various orchestral pieces.

This collection of poems represents an interpretation of autobiographical and biographical resources such as *Without Stopping* (autobiography of Paul Bowles); *An Invisible Spectator: A Biography of Paul Bowles,* Christopher Sawyer-Laucanno; *You Are Not I: A Portrait of Paul Bowles,* Millicent Dillon; as well as *Conversations with Paul Bowles*, edited by Gena Dagel Caponi; *In Touch: The Letters of Paul Bowles,* edited by Jeffrey Miller; *A Little Original Sin: The Life and Work of Jane Bowles,* Millicent Dillon. This collection is not a biography of Paul Frederick Bowles or Jane Auer Bowles.

# Acknowledgements

*Ars Poetica* (http://www.logolalia.com/arspoetica/ May 29, 2007) & *poem, home: An Anthology of Ars Poetica*, ed. Jennifer Hill & Dan Waber (Kingston, PA: Paper Kite Press, 2009) "Stories: On the Nature of Poetry."

*Contrarywise: An Anthology*, ed. Ruth Moon Kempher (St. Augustine, FL: Kings Estate Press, 2008): "Launch," "Riff on a Quarrelling Pair."

*Extract(s)* (http://dailydoseoflit.com/2012/06/01/excerpt-karen-alenier/): "Raconteurs in Tangier," "Flower: Paul's Love Song," "Exit Interview."

*Gargoyle* 59 (Arlington, VA: Paycock Press, 2013): "A College Boy Finds His Way," "Paris in the Twenties: 1929," "Bupple's Cat."

*The Innisfree Poetry Journal* (http://www.authorme.com/innisfree.htm) *Innisfree* 5: "Drawing Room Comedy." *Innisfree* 4: "Flower: Paul's Love Song," "Incisor," "An Onlooker Gossips," "The Parrot That Spoke to Jane Bowles," "Raconteurs in Tangier."

*Ocho* 23 (http://issuu.com/didimenendez/docs/ocho23 ): "Epiphany, Years Later: Jane Bowles Reminisces," "No Accident," "Strokes."

*On a Bed of Gardenias: Jane & Paul Bowles*, Karren LaLonde Alenier (Cleveland Heights, OH: Kattywompus Press, 2012): "Raconteurs in Tangier," "Incisor," "When Jane Met Paul," "Hidden Messages," "Yanked," "When You Crossed the Line," "The Parrot That Spoke to Jane Bowles," "Epiphany," "Riff on a Quarrelling Pair," "Launch," "Flower," "Recurring Dream of Paul Bowles," "Chasing the Fox," "Tongue-tied Tea," "The World Situation," "Here, Kitty," "Edge," "No Accident," "Gift," "Agonizer," "Drawing Room Comedy," "Strokes," "An Onlooker Gossips," "They Don't Like Burying Jews in Spain," "Stories: On the Nature of Poetry." "Exit Interview."

*The Poet and the Poem* Audio Podcast from the Library of Congress, 2004: (http://www.loc.gov/poetry/avfiles/Aleiner-Roberts-Solari-Tham.mp3) "Agonizer," "The Parrott That Spoke to Jane Bowles," "Raconteurs in Tangier."

*The Poet and the Poem* Audio Podcast from the Library of Congress, 2012: (http://www.loc.gov/poetry/poetpoem.html) "Terrorists," "Stories: On the Nature of Poetry," "Incisor," "When Jane Met Paul," "Hidden Messages," "Launch," "Flower: Paul's Love Song," "Exit Interview."

*Poetic Voices Without Borders 2*, ed. Robert L. Giron (Arlington, VA: Gival Press, 2009) "Edge," "When You Crossed the Line."

Poetrymagazine.com (March 2002): "From the Well."

*PoetryMagazine.com Anthology* (June 2014) "Hard to Resist."

*Poetry Repairs* (http://www.poetryrepairs.com/ ) *Repairs* 4: "Gift," *Repairs* 2: "When Jane Met Paul."

*Paul Bowles and Karren LaLonde Alenier, Tangier, 1982*

## About the Author

KARREN LALONDE ALENIER is the author of six previous collections of poetry, including *Looking for Divine Transportation* (The Bunny and the Crocodile Press), winner of the 2002 Towson University Prize for Literature. Her poetry and fiction have been published in such magazines as the *Mississippi Review*, *Jewish Currents*, and *Poet Lore*.

In 1982, through New York's School of Visual Arts, she worked with Paul Bowles in Tangier, Morocco, on her poems about Gertrude Stein. Some of these poems became part of her opera libretto on Stein.

*Gertrude Stein Invents a Jump Early On*, her jazz opera with composer William Banfield and Encompass New Opera Theatre artistic director Nancy Rhodes premiered at New York City's Symphony Space Leonard Nimoy Thalia in June 2005.

She writes feature articles and interviews, an arts blog called The Dressing, and a monthly column on Gertrude Stein for *Scene4 Magazine* at scene4.com. She is author of *The Steiny Road To Operadom: The Making Of American Operas*, a book about contemporary opera.

Since 2013, she has been leading an international online study group on Gertrude Stein's long poem *Tender Buttons*. The results of those in-depth studies can be seen on her blog at Alenier.blogspot.com.

She is a graduate of the University of Maryland College Park in French language and literature and a fellow of the Virginia Center for the Creative Arts. Since 1986, she has worked in a leadership role with the literary nonprofit The Word Works, promoting contemporary American poetry. She lives in Chevy Chase, Maryland, with her husband Jim Rich. She enjoys spending time with her son Ivan and his family in Middletown, New Jersey.

www.ingramcontent.com/pod-product-compliance
Lightning Source LLC
Chambersburg PA
CBHW021020090426
**42738CB00007B/849**